100

Days of Healing From Heartbreak

Suzi Sung

About the Author

After writing and releasing "100 days of Positivity, Hope and Growth" in 2020, Suzi Sung still isn't an internationally renowned author or a New York Times Best Seller. She's probably never going to climb Mount Everest (and has no plans to) and still hasn't got a degree... she barely even left the house last year!

She has, however, experienced heartbreak and she's here to tell you that "You don't know a bad haircut, until you get a good one." – and the same can be said for boyfriends too.

Oh... she also wrote this 2nd book.

Introduction

May this book calm you down when you are feeling anxious, comfort you when your friends can't be with you, heal you from the pain you're going through and remind you that you are f**king fabulous!

It's time to remember how badass you are.

The 5 Stages

1. Shock
2. Denial
3. Bargaining
4. Anger
5. Acceptance

The Shock Won't Last Forever

You've just gone through a breakup and you don't know what to do now, or how to fix things.

Your brain is trying to process a million thoughts and feelings at once.
Fear of being alone, questions about why this has happened, and what you will do now are running through your mind making it difficult to concentrate on anything.

Nothing is helping you make sense of the situation. You're left feeling lost and confused.

You're in shock.

Right now all of your emotions are coming over you at once and messing up your ability to rationalise.

When you feel like this, sometimes the best thing you can do is just ride it out.

Don't try to make any decisions today.

Allow yourself the time to jus
t be upset.
Let pain and all other emotions out and forget about the questions for today.

The emotional part of your brain is in the driver's seat right now, so if you try to think logically, it's going to be a struggle.

But that's okay.

Take comfort in knowing that this feeling of shock won't last forever, all the millions of thoughts running through your head will slow down and you will eventually be able to calm down.

Refrain yourself from making any rash decisions or doing anything drastic tonight.

Have a hot bath and try to get some sleep.

Your head will feel lighter in the morning once you've had some rest and you'll be able to process things more clearly.

You'll Feel Better In a Week

For all the breakups I have gone through, this is something that always gives me comfort.

You will feel better in a week!

I find the first week of being single again is always the most difficult because every experience is new and no one likes change, especially unexpected or unwanted change.

Waking up, feeling all alone, the absence of a "Good morning" text and not having that special someone to tell your day to can be overwhelming in the first week.

These things hurt because, as each new day begins, you think of how different it is compared to your last week when you were still in a relationship.

Don't worry, this is natural and it won't always feel so painful.

Once you get through the first week on your own, the second week becomes easier.

This is because you will have had some time to process your situation and get used to everything.

What you did last week will no longer be compared to a happier time. You'll be looking back at how shocked, upset, and low you were and you'll be grateful that you're no longer feeling as sad.

I have given this advice to so many friends of mine and it has never failed to work.

In the first week, you get used to waking up on your own and doing things by yourself. This will help you accept what has happened and get you used to your new routine.

Week One is like a practice run. By the time you get to Week Two, you'll know what to expect and be mentally prepared for it.

So, just focus on getting yourself through the first week the best you can, because the second week won't be as hard.

Oh Honey, You've Got This!

No matter how crappy and hopeless life feels right now, know that whatever you're going through, you *will* get through it.

You are a lot stronger than you think and this moment of doubt will pass.

If you're reading this book, then there is already a part of you that wants positive change and wants to feel better.

Know that you deserve to be happy and you already have the ability to get through anything, including this breakup.

So for the days where you feel like you don't believe in yourself, know that I believe in you.

Honey, you've got this!

Forget About the Big Stuff for Now

Right now, you may be thinking of all the different things you are going to have to deal with now that you're single.

You may be able to think more clearly, but that doesn't mean that your mind isn't still overrun with thoughts.

More specifically, all the challenges you now need to face.

How are you going to get over this?
Why did this happen?
What do you do now?
How are you going to tell everyone you're not together?
What will you do when you see your ex with someone else?
How will you meet someone new?

When I went through my breakup, I remember I worked myself up so much one day, that I could barely breathe. My heart was racing and my mind kept jumping quickly from thought to thought.

The pressure became so much that I burst into tears and I felt so lost in that moment that I wanted to give up.

Sounds dramatic, I know. But imagine you are a project manager and you have a team of people who all need something from you.

During a meeting, you let everyone speak to you at the same time.

Do you hear them all? Can you understand what they are saying? Are you able to help them?

Probably not, because so much is going on at one time, it's difficult to know where to start.

That's what it can be like when you put pressure on yourself to do everything at once.

I know that when you go through a breakup, you want to get over it quickly and you think by getting everything done, that will happen.

But it doesn't always work that way.

If you try to deal with every single worry, thought, or task straight away, you can end up more stressed as a result.

The best thing you can do right now is slow down and concentrate on one thing at a time if you're not feeling emotionally strong enough to handle the big stuff. Your only priority at this moment in time is to look after yourself and focus on getting to a point where you are ready to take the next step.

If you haven't even managed to get dressed today, it's unlikely you'll be in the right mindset to tell people you are now single. The best thing you can do is just work on getting to a place where you feel good enough to get out of your Pj's and get dressed.

Take it one step at a time. The more time you spend on feeling better about your situation, the easier it will be to deal with the big stuff.

You Won't Change His Mind—Only He Can Do That

Have you ever tried to persuade your ex to give your relationship another go? Promised that things will get better and that you can change? Or pleaded with him to rethink his decision?

I hate to be the one to tell you this, but if he has decided to end things, nothing you say or do will change his mind.

The only thing you can change is your own mindset.

Even if you did manage to convince him to give the relationship another go, would you be able to rest at night knowing that you had to beg and barter for someone to be with you?
As much as it may seem like a good idea right now to do whatever you can to get him back, so that you will feel better, it really won't help.

Don't waste your energy on a hopeless cause.

Spend your time on you and what you can do for your own life to get better.

Think of all the big promises you would make just to get your ex back. If you are willing to change so much of you just to make someone else happy, how much of that energy are you willing to put into changing things to make you happy?

That way, if he does end up coming back, you'll know he made the decision without any convincing.

You Are Enough!

Don't let the actions of one man make you doubt your own value.

He didn't let you go because you weren't attractive enough, funny enough, slim enough, smart enough or any other reason you might be thinking of.

You are more than enough just as you are and you shouldn't feel like you need to change yourself to make someone else happy.

If a guy can't see your value then he wasn't the right guy for you.

Don't torture yourself by thinking that the relationship ended because you weren't good enough.

You are not to blame for someone else's actions. You are more than worthy and you will find someone who deserves to be with you.

Have you ever thought he let you go because he was the one that wasn't enough?

Try to Resist the Temptation to Blow up His Phone

And I don't mean literally. Although, that's also tempting.

What I mean is try to avoid constantly calling or texting your ex for answers and ***do not*** tell them you want to get back together.
If they have made this decision, allow space to let it sink in for both of you.

Messaging or calling until he answers isn't going to get you anywhere and it won't make him want you back.
If anything, it can do the opposite.
Know the difference between fighting for someone you love and fighting for someone who doesn't want you to.

Respect the decision and give him time to process his own actions.
Imagine if you had ended a relationship and your ex kept calling, messaging and showing up at your door. How would it make you feel towards your ex?

Show your ex that you are mature enough to give him space, regardless of how you are feeling.

If he thinks you will do anything to get him back, he'll feel in control of the situation. As a result, he may not treat you with as much respect because he will think he can have you back whenever he wants. Give him a chance to feel what it's like to miss you. Let him think that you will be fine without him. Even if you don't feel that way right now.

When you do this, you let him see the strong, independent, capable side of you that can and will carry on whether he's in the picture or not.

Instead of letting him think you need him, let your actions remind him that you *chose* to be with him and that he was the lucky one.

So, even if you're finding it difficult to resist the temptation to call him and tell him how you feel, try to refrain from losing your cool. Not only will you take back your power and face the situation as equals, you won't have to look back and cringe at your actions in a few months' time.

Cry All You Want. Your Tears Will Dry Out Eventually

Have you ever heard someone who cried after a sad movie say they needed a good cry?
I get emotional from watching anything heartfelt. I am always the one in tears at the end and I don't mean cute cry tears. I mean full blown hysterics.

It might not look pretty, but it can feel pretty good afterwards.

Did you know that crying actually has a self soothing effect? It releases oxytocin (happy hormone) and endorphins (pain reliever)—chemicals that make people feel at ease physically and emotionally.
Not only that, your tears contain a number of stress hormones, so the more tears you shed, the more stress you release.

Some people find crying to be a weakness. If your concern right now is that crying means you are not strong or you're feeling frustrated that you can't stop crying over your ex.

Don't.

Let go of that guilt and just let the tears out.

Crying is a great emotional release and if your body's reaction to what you're going through is to cry, just let it happen.

You will eventually stop when you're too exhausted to continue; you won't feel so sad anymore.
Cry as much as you want to and let all the emotions out until you have nothing left.

You don't want to keep all the negative feelings in your body. If you can't release them, they will always be within you, waiting to resurface.

Let it all out now because you'll feel so much better in the long run.

Hitting Rock-bottom Isn't the End of the World

It can feel like your whole world is falling apart when you have just split from your partner and it seems like there is no hope for a happy future.

While this may be the end of the relationship, it's not the end of everything else, despite how it feels.

Whatever your circumstances are, know that you are not alone.
Sadly, there are many people just like you out there who are going through a breakup right this very moment and feeling the same way you are.

The thing is, As difficult as breakups can be, they can also be necessary.

Some people are not right for each other. However, they may only see it after the relationship has ended.

I remember feeling this way when I broke up with my ex.
I had hit a new level of heartbreak and when it finally got to the point when I felt things could not get any worse, that's when I knew that things would start getting better.

It can be difficult to see it at the time, but looking back now, I am grateful for the dark moments I went through because they made me into who I am now. I don't think I would have worked as hard to figure out what I really wanted in life had I not gotten to the point where I felt like I had no choice.

Here's the thing. You might be at an all-time low right now and you feel like you're not happy about anything in your life. It will force you to really think about what you really want. Most people are stuck in their comfort zones, meaning that they never really think outside the box when it comes to what they really want. They just accept the life that they have. You, on the other hand, have the opportunity to get creative and really think deeply about what you want the rest of your life to look like.

So, if today, you have hit your 'rock-bottom,' know that today is the day that things will start to improve. It may be a slow process, you may come across setbacks, and you'll probably feel like giving up at times, but if you can find a little bit of strength within you to decide that you are going to get through this, you will reach the top again.

Have Courage and Be Kick-ass!

Okay, so you didn't get your Cinderella fairytale with this guy.

I am truly sorry that you're having to go through this.

Believe me, I know how it feels.

Even though I don't know you, I do know that you are capable of anything, including getting past this period of sadness and getting over this breakup.

It might feel easier to play the victim, so to speak, but have you ever thought of the possibility of being the heroine in this story?

Sitting in your PJ's all day and eating ice cream while you watch Disney films may be useful for a time.

Eventually, it loses its appeal.

Only you can pull yourself out of this situation. Only you can choose to feel better.
Only you can decide that you are going to get over this.

Only you can save yourself.

There are times when it's right to act like a princess and there are times when it's right to be a superhero.

Now is the time to be the latter.

It's time to be strong and courageous and fight for a good cause (that cause being you).

Even though you feel sad and want to stay in bed all day, decide to have the courage to get up and do something.
Even though you're in pain right now, decide to work through it and heal from it.
Even though you don't feel worthy right now, decide that you're going to find your way back to feeling good enough again.
Once you've made these decisions, nothing will stop you.

Unleash the superwoman within you; be brave and tell yourself you will get through this.
You will get your power back and you will get your fairytale ending.

It's Okay to Be Sad, Just Don't Only Be Sad

You're going through a breakup. It's a crappy time and you have every right to be sad, but sadness doesn't have to be the only emotion you feel.
It will become too exhausting if you let it consume you and you'll have no energy for anything else.
So, whilst it's okay to be sad right now, Make sure to save some of your energy for other feelings too.

For example:

Be sad, but determined.

Determined to get through this.
Determined to get out of bed today.
Determined to go for that job you want.
Determined to smile at least once this week.
Determined to get out of the house and socialise.

Be sad, but grateful.

Grateful you had a lucky escape.
Grateful for the roof over your head.
Grateful for your friends and family's support.
Grateful that you still have a chance to find the right person.

Be sad, but hopeful.

Hopeful for better things to come.
Hopeful that this feeling won't last.
Hopeful that you're going to be okay.

Even though you are upset right now, you can still move forward, one small step at a time, by finding other feelings to put your energy towards.

When It Comes to 'Firsts,' Practice Makes Perfect

You know that moment when you are just waking from sleep?
For a split second, you forget that you're single again and then it hits you. Yes, the breakup did happen and yes, this is now your reality.

I used to find this difficult because every time I woke up, that realisation would take me back to the start when things first fell apart and those emotions came rushing back in.
Or, when you have to go to an event as a single girl for the first time—it can feel daunting.
Even doing your weekly food shopping by yourself can feel a bit strange at first.

Experiences like these can make it tough to wake up in the mornings, let alone get on with the rest of your day.

But that feeling will pass.

The first couple of weeks can be tough, but once you get over the 'first time' for doing something as a single person, you get used to it.

Then it gets to the point where you don't even think about these 'firsts' anymore. You just get on with your day-to-day life without comparing it to what you had.

As much as you may dread going through your 'firsts', know that each time you do, you are overcoming the fear.

The more you do it, the less you fear it, the easier it becomes.

Constant Contact Is Like Walking Around With a Stone in Your Shoe

Have you ever had a stone in your shoe while you were walking? That sharp pain hits the nerves in your foot and is so uncomfortable that you need to immediately stop walking, take off your shoe, and get rid of said stone. Now imagine that you feel another stone in your shoe, but instead of stopping, you continue to walk on it.

Each step brings you more pain and discomfort. It's difficult to imagine because who would choose to continue to feel pain when they don't have to?

Constant contact with an ex after a break-up is a bit like having a stone in your shoe. Every message you get from them is a constant reminder of what's happened. You miss them more and you want them more because you are reminded each day of what it was like to be together.

You might be thinking that you both are acting like you're back together so it must be a good thing. But if he's not saying he wants to be in a relationship with you again, then you're not together and the continual contact will prolong your suffering and stop you from moving forward.

I know that cutting contact will make things seem more real and you may not feel ready to do that. The longer you leave it, the more pain you'll feel and the longer it will take for you to heal from this.

I'm sure that deep down, you know it's true.

Take a moment to mentally prepare yourself. Then cut contact as if you're getting rid of that stone in your shoe and prepare to walk confidently and comfortably into your future.

If you try to cut contact and your ex refuses to accept it, try asking him what his intentions are and if he wants to be in a relationship again, then wait for an answer. If he doesn't tell you what you want to hear then there's no longer any need for you to speak.

You Are Going to Be Okay, Even if You Don't Believe It

Right now, you may feel like nothing is working out and you can't see yourself coming out of this situation in a better place.

That's just your fear and pain talking.

When you let your negative thoughts dominate your mind, it makes you focus more on the bad things that are happening. This makes it difficult to see or feel anything positive, thus making it harder to believe you will feel better.

When you feel this way, become more conscious of the fact that you're allowing negativity to take over.
By becoming more aware of your current emotions, you can begin to raise them to a more positive state.

When you have caught yourself in a negative thought pattern, say to yourself, "I am aware that I am being negative right now and it's making it difficult to believe things will get better, but I also know that I can change my thinking".

Choose to find an emotion that is more positive than the one you feel right now. It doesn't have to be positive, but just better than the one before.

Each time you do this, you will climb the ladder of emotions and eventually reach a positive one.

Don't forget. You are so strong, and so capable of doing anything and you will get through this.

Although you might not know why this is happening right now. Time really does heal and eventually you'll be able to look back on this moment and understand why it happened.

Do what you can to feel a slightly better emotion than you feel right now and try to have a good day.

When you make the decision to feel better, you will.

You'll Get Sick of Feeling Sad

Breakups are difficult and while there is no timeframe on how long it'll take to get over it, You will get to a point where you just physically and mentally don't want to feel sad anymore.
Feeling miserable everyday is exhausting. We were not put on this planet to feel low all of the time. Although, right now feeling sad seems easier than feeling happy. The tables will turn and there will be a shift.
Your emotions affect you physically and your body feels your pain as much as you do, but it doesn't want to feel tense and uncomfortable all the time. It'll get to a point where being sad takes more effort and energy than being happy.

You will feel so exhausted but you won't know it because you'll be so used to carrying the weight of sadness until one day something happens and you remember how good it feels to feel good.

For me, it was sitting in my work bestie's car on our lunch break listening to old school RnB music and laughing at each other for getting caught dancing in our seats by someone passing.

I had felt so upset for so long. I was waking up everyday feeling so sad and upset about my situation.

That was until this day.

I remember laughing so hard that I couldn't breathe and feeling so happy in that moment that I forgot about my heartbreak.

That's when it hit me.

I was so over being sad and I was ready to feel good again.

Once I decided that I was ready to feel good again, my days started to get easier and easier. Then one day, I realised I was no longer sad. I was over that period in my life and I had gotten to the point where I was happy again.

And that felt good.

Please know that despite how sad you may be feeling right now, once you remember what it's like to laugh and be happy again, you won't let sadness control your days any longer.

There Will Come a Day Where You Don't Think About Them

Do you find that every spare moment you have to think is filled with your ex?

I found this for a while after my breakup.
My day would be consumed with memories of the things we did, conversations we had, and daydreaming of what could have been.

It got to the point where I couldn't get to sleep at night because I'd replay conversations that we had in my head and then my mind would be obsessed with what would have happened if I had said something different.

Replaying these situations is pointless in the sense that you cannot change the past. All this does is add to the pain and leave you wishing for a time machine.
If your situation is anything like this or if you're sick of your ex running about in your head all the time. Just make sure you know that it won't last forever and that you do things to take your mind off of them.

Fill your day with things that keep you busy and distracted. You'll start to think less and less about him. Watch a movie, read a book, hang out with friends, or start that new business venture. Whatever it is you choose to do, make it something fun—something that requires your full attention so that you have no time to think about anything or anyone else. When you take the focus off of him and start to pay attention to your own needs, you'll start to do things that make you happy.

You'll start to enjoy your life again.

Keep yourself so busy doing what you love because one day you'll be doing something random and you'll realise that you're no longer thinking about your ex and what he's up to.

And trust me, that is something to feel good about.

Logic > Emotion

We all know it's easy to let our emotions take over and block out any form of logic from our brain. When you're feeling a bit stronger in yourself and you're ready for a different perspective.

Ask yourself the following questions about the person you were in a relationship with.
I'd like you to give two answers to each question. One should be if they made you feel this way in the past and the second should be if they are making you feel this way now, in the present.

Did/Does he make you want to become a better person?
Did/Does he make your life feel richer?
Did/Does he make your life easier?
Did/Does he make you happier?

For the present questions, base it on what you actually feel and what is actually happening right now,. rather Rather than on what you would feel *if* he did certain things.

Now that you've done this exercise, take a look at your answers. You'll probably see that the majority of 'yes' answers will be in the past rather than the present.

If you are ready to let logic speak to you, you'll realise that what once made you happy, no longer does.

It's okay ok to let it go now because it's something that no longer serves you.

Let's Make a List

Legit, this isn't a quote. This is a task.

My friend did this for me once when I was upset over a breakup. Afterwards, I instantly felt more reassured that I was going to be okay.

I hope this works for you.

Write a list of all the qualities you would like in your soulmate. Be specific. And honest!

Once you're done, take a good look at this list.

Was your ex everything on your list?

No?

Mine wasn't either.

But you know what that means, right?

It means that this ex wasn't everything you wanted from a partner and now that you are no longer together you have a greater chance of meeting this guy on your list.

And when you do, you're going to be so glad things didn't work out with your ex.

This exercise will not only make you feel better, but taking time to be honest about your ex partner will help you see that they weren't 'all that.' You can also take comfort in knowing that the things that used to annoy you about them are no longer your problem.

You wanna know the most amazing thing?

A week after I wrote this list, an old flame I used to date got in touch and asked me out. Some of the qualities on my list were actually based on him!

I'm not saying that will definitely happen as quickly for you, but know that it **can** happen.

When You Move Onto Anger, You Can Begin to Move On

I always feel relief when I get to this stage of a breakup.
Why?
Well, for a start, it means I'm no longer sad.
I am pissed!
This is the part of a breakup where you're filled with energy and fire and you want to show him what a big mistake he made by letting you go.

You want to get even—and you can.

Now, I don't mean go out and key his car, trash his house, or find a new boyfriend to rub in his face.

The best way to get even is to get on great without him.

After a breakup, I go on a mission to look and feel as good as I can.
For me, it involves getting fit and healthy. Changing my hair colour, reorganising my wardrobe, my life and also, some serious retail therapy.

My theory behind it is that I will look so damn good, he'll wish he never let me go. When that time comes, I'll be able to tell him where to shove it (FYI, this has never happened).

That's the angry part of me that wants revenge. I'm a Scorpio; I was born vengeful. The thought of getting my 'revenge' keeps me going and gives me the determination to succeed at whatever goal I have set for myself.

Take the energy from your newfound anger and pour it into something productive, whether it be joining a new boxing class, making plans to go out and socialise more, putting in more effort at work, or even quitting your job to go for your dream job.
Do whatever it is that you have always wanted to do and do it at full force.
Do it with so much energy, fire, and passion that you become completely focussed on reaching your goal.
Even if you're doing it for the wrong reasons at the start, your anger will fade. The need for revenge will be gone and you'll find that you have become an even better version of you in the process.

When You Are Stuck Between Resentment and a Hard Place, Free Yourself With Forgiveness

Resentment. Easy to recognise. Not so easy to remove.

If you're feeling resentment towards your ex and know you won't get the explanation or apology you would like, it can leave you a bit stuck when it comes to letting go and moving on. The anger and annoyance can eat away at you and keep you trapped and unable to move past this stage.

When I've been in this situation, most of the time I would try and block it out or completely cut the person out of my life. Even though, deep down it wasn't what I wanted. I would get over it eventually, but the suffering I endured left me pretty emotionally drained.

Then one year ago, I had an epiphany.

It was New Years Eve. I was writing out my New Year's resolutions when I realised that I didn't want to start the new year still holding on to resentment and anger towards anyone.
I realised that I had wasted all my energy on an emotion that I didn't even want to feel. I had known for a while that I wasn't going to get an explanation,

apology, or closure regarding the situation. It wasn't until that very moment that I truly accepted it, and by doing so, I released the resentment and instantly felt better.

I made a decision to no longer question why things happened the way they did or why this person treated me the way they did. I chose to let it be and accepted that people are the way they are.

Once I made this decision, I honestly felt as if the resentment left my body. My energy shifted and I instantly felt lighter. I was happier and more hopeful. I had freed up space to feel better.

When you let resentment consume you, it doesn't leave much room for any other feelings.

If you're in a situation where you know you won't get an explanation, instead of letting that annoyance get to you, try accepting and forgiving it. Once you have, you'll be able to release your resentment and allow space to feel good again.

You Might Be Suffering Now, But He'll Feel It in the Long Run

It might feel like you're the only one who's hurting right now.

And, it's probably partly true.

Do you feel like your ex is having the time of his life now that he's single? While you're still trying to come to terms with everything?

I know it sucks and you're no doubt wondering why you're hurting and he isn't, but people deal with breakups in different ways.

Men have a tendency to throw themselves back out into the world like nothing ever happened.

It might look like they are enjoying their freedom and loving their life without you.
But the truth is, a lot of men block out their feelings after a breakup. Instead of dealing with their emotions, They drown them out with distractions like work, drinking, and partying.
On the outside, it looks as though they are completely carefree and emotionless.
They will be trying to convince themselves that they made the right decision and that they are doing fine without you.

But after a few months, once all the alcohol and partying is out of their system, they will feel it.

They'll go through the same pain you're going through right now. They'll miss you like you're missing them right now and they'll also have to go through the whole healing process that you're going through.

The only difference is that when they're suffering, you will have already moved on from that stage and be in a much better place than he is.

So, if it seems like your ex is already over you when you've only just broken up, rest assured.
He hasn't even reached that stage yet. And when he does, he'll really know what it feels like to have his ex move on from him.

Sometimes Bad Things Have to Happen So That You Can Grow

I truly believe that if everything was good in your life all the time then you would never learn to grow as a person.
If everything in your life was always how you wanted it to be, then you would never feel the need to change.

And if you never change, you'll never grow.

I had an opportunity to stay in Canada for longer if I really wanted to. However, at the time I was in a long distance relationship and had decided that after my visa was up, I would come home and start my life with this person.

I quit my job, cancelled the lease on my apartment, and booked my flight back to the UK. I was ready to come home and start a new chapter of my life in England.
Two weeks before I was due to come home, my boyfriend at the time ended things unexpectedly and with no explanation.

By this point, it was too late to make arrangements to stay in Canada so I had to move back to Scotland, which was something I had not planned for.

I had to start all over again. Single, jobless, and back at my gran's house.

Do I regret it?

I can honestly say that I don't.
Do I miss living abroad? Definitely.
Do I wish I was still living there? Absolutely!
But do I regret the choices I've made? No chance in hell!
Why? Because the drastic change in my circumstances made me learn a lot about who I was as a person and helped me to grow into a better version of me.

If I didn't come home when I did, I wouldn't have written my first book, *100 Days of Positivity, Hope and Growth*.
This book helped to heal me in so many ways. It made me realise my true life goal is to help and inspire others to follow their dreams.

I think if I had stayed in Canada, I would not have become the person that I am today.

There are so many other reasons too, but I won't bore you with all the details.
All I can say is if you're wondering why these bad things have happened to you. Just know there is a good reason for it all.

Even if you don't know what it is right now, you ***will*** find out eventually.

So in the meantime, just keep doing what you can to be happy in this present moment.

The Longer You Stay in Denial, the Longer It'll Take to Feel Better

What is going on?
This is a joke right?
This isn't real is it?
What did I do wrong?
I thought he loved me?
Did this really just happen?
Surely not, am I dreaming?

You may feel like you won't be able to move on until you get the answers to these questions. However, these questions are actually the reason why you're not getting anywhere.

They all represent a form of denial and when you stay in denial of a situation, that numbness and detachment from your current reality is holding you back from moving on to the next stage of the breakup.

I know that emotions can take hold and it makes it all the more confusing. The same thoughts go round and round in your head, yet you can't seem to get clarity.

Deep down, you already know the answers to these questions. So the real question here is, are you ready to face them?

What is going on?	*Your relationship just ended.*
This is a joke right?	*Unfortunately, no.*
This isn't real is it?	*Very real.*
What did I do wrong?	*Nothing. Sometimes these things just happen.*
I thought he loved me?	*I'm sure he did and you know that.*
Did this really just happen?	*Yes it did, but you're going to be okay.*
Surely not, am I dreaming?	*Again, nope. The sooner you accept it, the sooner you can work on feeling better.*

Resisting Change = More Suffering

This fact isn't just for breakups. It works with everything in life.

Imagine that your life is like swimming down a stream.
When something happens that causes unwanted or unexpected change, and you add resistance to that change, It's like deciding to try and swim back upstream. If you've ever tried to swim against the current, you'll know it's much more difficult than swimming with the flow. You don't get very far and sometimes you end up staying in the same place because with every forward stroke you take, the water takes you back one.
It keeps you fixed in one place and this is exactly what happens when you try to fight against the changes happening in your life right now.
You can't go back. But because you won't move forward, you end up keeping yourself stuck in the same cycle of suffering.

The best thing you can do in this scenario is go with the flow of the steam. In other words, go with the change that is happening. Afterall, if you can't change it, you might as well change with it.

Regardless of the type of breakup you're going through, One fact is inevitable... *change is going to happen.*

Whether it's getting used to having to move out of the place you once called home, spending your weekends on your own, the end of couples nights, or having someone to kill the spiders in the house.
Things are not going to be the same.
Rather than putting yourself through the torment of wishing things were how they used to be, knowing fine well they won't ever be again, try to embrace it and let your newfound freedom empower you instead of upset you.

So you had to move out of your "home"; now you get to make a new place your home.
Now you spend your weekends on your own; that just means more 'me time'.
It's the end of couples nights; and the start of 'Girls Night'.
Which, let's face it, is always more fun anyways!
That just leaves the spiders; unfortunately this is just something you're going to have to get used to. But you get my point, right?

If things are going to have to change, you might as well make the most of these changes by paying attention to the good things it will bring.
Most people have to go through some form of hardship in their lives, but it usually takes them to

an even better place. When you stop trying to swim upstream, you let it take you to the even better place much quicker.

If He Wants to Text You, He Will Find a Way

"He lost his phone".

"His phone has no signal".

"He's waiting for the right moment".

"Maybe he's been really stressed with work".

"He's probably busy trying to sort his head out so we can get back together".

"He wants to get in touch but he's afraid because he thinks I won't hear him out".

Whatever reason you tell yourself for why you haven't heard from him, know this:

If a guy wants to talk to you, he will get in touch.

Don't waste any more time convincing yourself there's a reasonable explanation for why his name hasn't flashed up on your phone yet.

If he wants to contact you, nothing will stop him.

Accept and Accelerate Out of Your Comfort Zone

The shock of a breakup is undeniable. Sometimes that shock and the realisation that your life is about to change can feel like too much. You are thrown out of your comfort zone and when that happens, you automatically want to get back into it. This is one of the reasons why when a breakup happens, you will want to get back with that person, even when you know it's never going to happen or when you are the one doing the dumping.

It's like a reflex.

Our brains want us to stay in our comfort zone because it is safe and there is less risk of experiencing emotional hurt.

When you step out of it, it does what it can to make you stay in there.

Your brain puts all of your focus on trying to get your ex back and get back into your comfortable place, while ignoring anything that contradicts this goal.

It stops you from being able to see any options that will keep you out of your comfort zone, even if it is something that would do you good.

If you were to see these options, you might want to stay outside of your comfort zone and your natural instinct is not to do that.

It's hard to get your head in gear and figure out your next moves when you are unable to accept the situation for what it is.

When this happens, denial slams on the breaks and stops your progress.
The only way you will be able to release the brakes is by letting go of your denial and accepting what is going on right now—instead of fighting for what used to be.

When one of the relationships I was in had ended, all I could think about was how I might be able to make it work and how to get my ex back. The reality was that it was over and there was no going back, but denial meant that I wasn't willing to move forward, So I was stuck.
It wasn't until I was willing to accept that I was single again, that I was able to see the other options available for me to get myself back on track.

I'm not saying that you will never get back with your ex because every situation is different. However, if right now that is not an option, no matter how much you try, then the best thing you can do to feel better is to accept it.

Once you accept it, you will release the brakes and begin to accelerate out of your comfort zone.

Don't Torture Yourself Unnecessarily

Social media has become a great platform for connecting with people and seeing what your friends are up to.

It's also great for snooping.

Now I'll be honest, I've never been much of a snooper myself. The last thing I want to be doing when I'm trying to get over someone is seeing everything they're up to!

But I know, for some of you ladies out there, it's not so easy to step away from the profile.

I've witnessed first-hand experience of this from several of my friends, who I now believe would have had great careers as government spies.

You may think that knowing what they are up to may bring you comfort, especially if you notice that they haven't posted anything since you broke up.

But have you thought about what happens if you do see something you don't want to?

How would it make you feel?

Would you feel strong enough to handle it right now?
Or, would it make you jump five steps back in your own progress?

I know, not everyone will take this advice, but I hope some of you do because it *will* help.

Try to refrain from snooping on your ex whilst you're still recovering from your breakup. Make your day too fun and interesting, so you never feel the need to know what he is up to. Remember, you might be hurt by what you see.

Get yourself to the point where you're so happy and so over it that if you were to look at your ex's Instagram, anything you saw wouldn't phase you.

Save yourself the torture and leave the snooping to him.
I promise, you'll thank me for it one day.

Do You Have Protection?

Have you ever looked back on guys you've dated in the past and thought, thank God I didn't end up with him! Even though, at the time, you wished it had worked out.

Well, have you ever thought that one day you'll feel the same way about this ex?

I know, I know, this guy is different, right? I have no doubt he is, and maybe you will be together one day, but right now if it's not happening, try not to spend all day questioning why.

Have you ever thought that somehow the universe is trying to protect you from making the wrong choices in your life?

Maybe the timing just isn't right. Maybe there's still more work for you to do before you settle down with the right one. Maybe this has happened because you still have things to learn and this experience is necessary for you to grow.
Or maybe there is someone even better out there for you.

My dad fell in love with my stepmom 30 years ago when I was just born and when he was still married to my mum.

Although they were madly in love, they decided for the sake of his marriage to go their separate ways.

Fast forward to today and they are now happily married after reconnecting a few years ago.
I asked my stepmom if she ever wished that she had stayed with my dad all those years ago, as it was clear they were meant for each other.
"Definitely not," she replied. Because if she had stayed with my dad back then, she would never have met her late husband, which meant she wouldn't have had her two daughters whom she loves dearly and can't imagine life without.

You don't know what your future holds or what the universe is protecting you from right now.
So, as frustrating as it is, try not to question everything that is happening and stressing over something that can't be changed.

Trust that everything is happening for you, even if it doesn't feel like it right now.

Anytime you feel negatively towards a situation that cannot be changed, tell yourself you are being protected. It always gives me comfort and always turns out to be true.

Once You Realise He's Not Coming Back, You'll Make Your Comeback

There's always that little bit of hope that your ex is going to come knocking on your door asking for forgiveness and begging you to take him back.

Holding on to this hope can stop you from moving on with your own life.
It's so easy to put yourself on hold because part of you is waiting for this to happen.
But you end up stuck on heartbreak because you're stuck on the idea of a reconciliation that may never happen.

Then there will come a day when it hits you.

The moment when you realise that he's *not* coming back for you.

Whether it's after seeing his new girlfriend on his Instagram or hearing that he's doing fine without you, That moment will come and when it does, it may hurt.

You might feel surprised and shaken by this, but the shock will also shock you into acceptance.
It will make you realise that your ex isn't coming back to you and you'll let go of the tiny bit of hope you were still holding on to.

When this happened to me, I was upset at first. It's never nice to know that someone has moved on when you're still missing them. But it forced me to face the fact that it was completely over and that it was time to let go of that part of my life.

When I was finally honest with myself about the situation, I felt liberated and empowered. I knew at that point that this guy could not be for me. If he was, we would be together. I gave up on that tiny bit of hope I was still holding onto and was able to put all my love and energy into me, myself and I. This is when I really began to grow and I started to really work towards the life I wanted.

when this happens to you, embrace it and feel good about releasing an idea that isn't working for you.

When you do, that's when you'll make your comeback.

Treat Yourself Today, You Deserve It!

When was the last time you did something just for you?

When you're in a relationship, a lot of the time, it's about compromising so that both parties are happy. But now you're on your own, take some 'me time' and do the things you love that make you feel good.

Spend that extra time in the shower. Have a girly pamper day. Take up all the room in the bed. Have ice cream for breakfast. Buy that top you've had your eye on.

Whatever it is, do something to treat yourself for getting this far and being so strong.

You may have a long way to go in getting over your ex, but that doesn't mean it has to be doom and gloom all the time.

Take a day off from being heartbroken.

Go do something fun. Treat yourself to something pretty that makes you feel good—you deserve it!

No More Sad Songs!

Research has found that music activates parts of your brain that deals with emotions. The type of music you listen to can affect your mood and even how you perceive a situation.

If you're listening to sad songs all the time, know that this won't be helping you move on. If anything, it will intensify your emotions, making you feel even worse.

Time to skip the sad songs about heartbreak, deception and sad times.
Find something more upbeat.
For me, it wasn't happy songs as much as empowering ones that said f**k you, watch what I can do!

Here are a few of my favourites that really got me motivated and feeling good.

Warning: My choices are probably pretty dated and not cool, but do what works for you.

Little Mix - Hair
Taylor Swift - ME!
Clean Bandit - Tears

Dua Lipa - New Rules
Beyoncé - Irreplaceable
Ariana Grande - Problem
Destiny's Child - Survivor
Demi Lovato - Skyscraper
Mariah Carey - Shake it Off
Justin Beiber - Love Yourself
Little Mix - Shout Out To My Ex
Taylor Swift - Look What You Made Me Do
Justin Timberlake - What Goes Around... Comes Around

Put a pause on those emotional ballads and play some feel good music instead.

Realising The Truth About You and Him

Not Everything Happens For a Reason, But Breakups Do

When you're blindsided by a breakup you didn't see coming it can feel so confusing.

You feel lost and keep questioning why it happened. Everything seemed so perfect, or at least it does now that it's over.
We have a tendency to put our relationships on pedestals once they've ended.

Only thinking about the good stuff makes you paint a romanticised picture of what your relationship was like.

It makes you forget about all the bad stuff that helps you see that the reality was quite different.

When it's fresh, your emotions can mask your judgement. You end up only remembering the good things about a person and why you miss them.

Once your head is in a clearer space, you'll be able to look at the facts for what they are and you may realise that the relationship wasn't as perfect as you once thought.

If it was, you would still be together.

Don't Fear Being Alone, Fear Ending up With the Wrong Person

You know the saying, "You only remember the good things about someone when they're gone?"

Well, fear of being alone can do the same thing.

When you're newly single, it can be hard to accept at first and it's tough doing everything by yourself when you're so used to having someone there.
But don't let that hide you from the truth and paint your ex as your perfect man. If he was, your relationship would have worked out.

I'm not saying that this person will never be right for you , but if the relationship is over, then *something* wasn't right and remembering that will help you accept what has happened. Only then can you begin to move forward.

So many couples stay together, even when they're not entirely happy, because they fear being alone. They might even know deep down that this person isn't right for them, but they let their fear stop them from making the right decision.

By doing this, they miss out on the chance to find someone who is truly right for them and waste their time in a mediocre relationship.

In other words, they choose to settle for *anyone* rather than no one.

Don't let the fear of being alone make you think that you want your ex back for the wrong reasons Because you could miss out in the long run.

You won't be alone forever, but if you choose to settle instead of waiting for the right person, you will always feel unfulfilled in your relationships.

Maybe He's the One Who Cheated, but He Only Cheated Himself

If your ex cheated on you, I'm so sorry.
That sucks and you don't deserve that—no one does.

I've been there before and I know the shock, hurt and anger can be overwhelming.

Please know that you are not to blame for this. You did **not** do anything wrong and there was nothing you could have done to prevent this.

Cheating is a choice, not an accident. Replaying how you could have prevented it is pointless because it would have happened sooner or later.

I'm sure, whoever you are, that you're an amazing woman who was also an excellent girlfriend to a man who didn't deserve you.

It is extremely common to feel insecure and unworthy when you've been cheated on, and although right now you may feel like you've lost the relationship battle, he's the real loser in this.

Take comfort in knowing that one day he will regret it. By that point, you'll have forgotten who he is.

Are You Ready to Face the Facts?

When you feel ready to really face the truth of your relationship and why it broke down, these are the questions to ask yourself.

Warning: This may feel uncomfortable, having to face the truth of who you are or who your ex was can be challenging and it can stir up some unwanted emotions.

However, like I said in my last book, *100 Days of Positivity, Hope and Growth*, "You Can't Have Growth Without Growing Pains".

Therefore, whilst most people may want to skip this part, know that by doing it, you will be strengthening your self awareness and giving in to real growth.

What did you learn from this relationship?
Was there anything you could have done differently?
Were you completely satisfied with the relationship?
Did you ignore warning signs that this relationship wasn't right?
How did you feel when there was conflict and how did you react?
What would you want in your next relationship that this one didn't have?

Is there anything you'd like to change about how you handled the situation?
Did this person bring out the best in you and did you bring out the best in him?

When I had to face the facts of my relationship, I understood that my ex wasn't the only one at fault.

I should have walked away long before it ended because deep down, I knew it wasn't right. I ignored my gut feelings and listened to my ego instead. My ego told me that I was at the age for settling down, I'm getting too old to meet someone new, and this was as good as it's going to get. As a result, I wasted more time and energy on something that was only half fulfilling.

I made choices that I would never have made if I was more honest about my relationship at the time. It was a hard pill to swallow at first. However, once I worked through it, I was able to move on. I could forgive myself and let go of the guilt I was harbouring about the bad decisions I'd made.

So, even though it may be hard to deal with, know that when you can really let go, that's when you really grow.

When You Can't Get Closure, Close the Door

GHOSTING: *When a person cuts off all communication with their friends or the person they're dating, with zero warning or notice beforehand.*

Breakups are hard enough just as they are, but breakups that happen with no real explanation can be even worse.

'Ghosting' has become such a common occurrence that it even appears in the Urban Dictionary.

Not having any idea what happened and being completely ignored is never going to feel nice, but don't let it take away all of your self confidence.
Not being given a real explanation, or being ghosted by an ex, has nothing to do with who you are and everything to do with who they are.
If this has happened to you, know that your ex (or whoever you were dating) is being a coward. They are too afraid to be upfront and honest with you so they choose the easy way out.

I don't know about you, but I find people like this *super* unattractive.

If this has happened to you, put yourself in the other person's shoes and ask yourself what type of person you need to be, to be so inconsiderate.
It might make you realise how unworthy of you this person is and even put you off them.

Try to let go of the need for a detailed explanation of what happened, or even a reply, and turn your focus onto your own needs.
Keep in mind, you might not get the closure you were looking for. The silence that comes from ghosting speaks volumes to you.

Your answers may come in time.

For now, shut that door.

You know what they say—when one door closes, another one opens.

When You Stop Asking Why? You Can Start Asking What?

Why did this happen?
Why didn't he want me?
Why didn't I see the signs?
Why didn't it work out?

These questions, whilst understandable after a breakup, aren't very productive.
It can feel like you need to know the answers because you think it will make you feel better, and sometimes it can. But also know that if you're not going to get the answers you want, it's more productive to ask "What?" instead.

These questions are **way** more useful.

What should I do now?
What do I want for me?
What is my next step?
What makes me happy?

So, when you're done with asking yourself "why", start to ask yourself "what" instead.

Once you've got your answers, you can start to make new plans that don't involve your ex and the "why" questions will no longer matter.

Sometimes They Come Back but That's Not Always a Good Thing

Has he been in touch? Were you kind of happy when you got the text? Did you call all your friends to discuss what exactly he meant when he texted to say, "Hi, how are you?"

If your ex comes back into your life after cutting contact, it can stir up a lot of mixed emotions.
It may come as excitement, fear, joy, or confusion. Whatever you are feeling, ask yourself honestly, what do you want from this?

Are you in a good place now and are you happy, or do you still miss him?

Just as importantly, find out why he is in touch with you again.

Does he want you back?
Does he know he made a mistake?
Does he feel lonely and only wants an ego boost or a booty call?

Sorry, I had to say it.

Sometimes exes come back into your life because they've realised what a big mistake they've made. If that's the case, and you want him back, go for it.

If he's not on his knees begging for forgiveness, and for you to give him another chance, Have a good think about what it is he's after.

Did he go out into the big bad world of dating and realise that it's not so easy?
Does he feel lonely and wants to have some easy company for the night?
Maybe he does miss you, but does he want you back or does he just want sex?

More importantly, does having him in your life again work for you?

As I said, sometimes exes come back, but it's not always a good thing. Find out if you're his 'one and only' or his 'one night only' before you let him in again.

What Are Your Ex-Pectations?

Did you break up with your ex, but you're still seeing each other/sleeping together?

This happens quite a lot. In my experience, someone always ends up getting hurt in the long run.

So, if you are still seeing your ex, ask yourself and him, what outcome you both expect.

Are you still seeing him, in the hopes that he'll realise what he's lost and want you back?
Or did you do the breaking up and you're not quite ready to let go, but you don't want him back?

If you want to get back together with your ex, Giving him your time, your energy, and a good time after a breakup, is not the way to get him back.

Trust me on this.

You're giving him all the good stuff without any of the emotional responsibility that comes with being in a relationship.

In other words, your feelings might not be considered.

Whilst you think you're on the road to getting back together, he's maybe thinking he's won the jackpot.

Sex and attention with no actual commitment.

If it's the other way around, then have a think about what your actions could be doing to the other person.

Either way, make sure you're both on the same page.

If you're not, one of you is going to be very disappointed in the end.

He Might Miss You but It Doesn't Mean Anything if He Does Nothing About It

I'm sure your ex is missing you. It's not easy to erase someone out of your memory completely (though I have wished I could at times).

The thing is, even though you think your ex is missing you or if he's telling you he misses you, It doesn't mean anything unless he's doing something about it.

Missing someone and making a choice to be with them are two different things.
Try not to confuse them both.

If your ex is telling you he misses you, but he isn't telling you he wants to get back together, don't hold on to his words and give yourself false hope.

Remember when someone says something you want to hear, but doesn't take any action, their words are just *empty air.*

Keep yourself busy and don't give him too much of your time whilst you're trying to heal from this breakup, especially not until you know what his intentions are.

Keep moving forward and keep doing things that better your own life without him.

Let him miss you enough for him to come back to you with a real offer of commitment.

If he doesn't, at least you won't have wasted your time waiting for him to come around.

When a Guy Is Unsure of What He Wants, Don't Be His Backup Plan

If your ex is telling you that he loves you, but he's just confused or he's being indecisive about what he wants, don't sit around and wait for him to decide because it might never happen.
No matter what the reason is, whether he is going through a bad time or having to deal with personal issues, that should not get in the way of you two being in a relationship.

Have you told him that you will stick by him regardless, because you know you can both make it work and he still is unsure?

Then you have your answer.

Don't wait around for him to decide whether he wants to be with you or not.

If he doesn't know the answer, he's not ready or worthy of you right now.

For all you know, he could be dating other girls too and keeping you there in case it doesn't work out with them. (Who wouldn't want to have a backup person for when things go wrong?)

Guys can be pretty selfish and will leave you hanging as long as they can because they want to know you're there just in case they realise they can't do any better.

If your ex is unsure, leave him to it.
That's his problem.
You are too valuable a woman to sit about and wait for some guy to figure out what he wants.

Remember that regardless of your situation, he made the choice to not be with you.

You are the end goal, not his back up plan, so start acting like it.

Are You Listening to Your Heart or Your Ego?

Ask yourself, why are you really upset right now?

Is it because you've lost the love of your life or is it just that you no longer have someone?

Some people stay in relationships longer than they should because of insecurity and fear of being alone.
Other people take longer getting over a breakup than they should because of rejection or a bruised ego and not because they truly miss their ex.

Now this isn't always the case, but before you subject yourself to months of feeling heartbroken and sad, Be honest about why you feel this way.

Are you hurt because you miss your ex or is your ego hurting because someone out there doesn't want to be with you?

This may make you realise that the real reason you're upset is really because you feel rejected by this person and not because you think you've lost 'the one'.

When you can distinguish between the two, you will be able to look at the relationship more logically.

You'll stop romanticising it and instead see it for how it really was.

Be honest, is it your heart or your ego that is hurting?

It's Really Not You, It's Him

If a man can't see how amazing you are and that he would be lucky to have you, it is *not your job* to convince him.

A smart man knows when he's got something good and he won't let it go.

Don't ever feel like you need to show someone that you are worthy of them.

You are already worthy as you are and if he doesn't see that, then that's his problem.

So many girls are left wondering what is wrong with them whenever a relationship breaks down or a guy no longer wants to see them.

We automatically start blaming ourselves and pick out every little imperfection we have. We convince ourselves that if we were just a little bit skinnier, prettier or sexier, then maybe he wouldn't have left.

I have had so many friends ask me what's wrong with them when this happens and the answer is always the same, "NOTHING".

There is nothing wrong with you and if you did your best in the relationship then that was good enough.

Don't let your self worth come into question because some guy cannot be the man you deserve.

That is not your problem. Ever.

If a guy gives you the classic, "It's not you, it's me" line, Take his word for it and be glad you don't need to deal with his issues.

Just Because Someone's Great, Doesn't Mean They Are Great for You

Sometimes relationships just don't work out—even when no party is at fault.

It's sad, but it happens.

The hard part is dealing with it when it happens to you.

Missing someone that you can't say anything bad about makes it all that more difficult to move on. When you go through a bad breakup with someone you know wasn't worthy, it's much easier to believe you'll find someone better.

But what do you tell yourself when your ex is a great guy?

Here's my Answer:

He may have been a great guy, but that doesn't mean he's the right one for you.

There will be someone out there who is better suited to you, even though it might not seem like it right now.

Once you're willing to believe it, that's when you'll be open to seeing other great guys out there in the world.

Don't settle for someone just because you don't think you can get any better.

If it's not right, it's not right—no matter how many boxes they may tick.

He Really Wasn't Perfect After All

Have you had that lightbulb moment yet?

You know the one, where you realise your ex was not the perfect man.

If you haven't had this yet, don't worry, you will. And it will feel bloody brilliant!

When you start the healing process, you also start to see things more clearly for what they were, rather than what you thought they were.

Maybe it's the time he was in a mood over nothing major and caused a big argument, The fact that he didn't like to try new things, Or that he was a very fussy eater.

Whatever the reason, you'll begin to remember the little things that you didn't like about your ex, but you disregarded because you really liked him at the time.

Well when that time is over, you'll realise that he wasn't actually *that great* after all.

When you get to this stage, you'll stop thinking your ex was perfect.
You might realise he wasn't that great after all.

That thought alone might make you realise you don't actually want him back.

And then, you'll be over him.

You've Got Enough Facebook Friends!

Holiday seasons and birthdays are a great way to get in touch with someone that you've wanted to speak to for a while and have been unsure how to start the conversation. However, If your ex messages and then vanishes once you've replied, until the next yearly holiday event comes along, then there's a good chance he's doing it for selfish reasons.

Cutting contact is effective because it allows you to move on without a constant reminder of the past. Something as small as a "Merry Christmas" text message can set you back five steps if you don't see it for what it really is.

Girls will read into messages like this for hours, wondering what it all means, asking friends what they think, and how they should reply (be honest, we've all been there).

It can be disappointing if you reply, only to realise that the message meant nothing.
If part of you still wants your ex to come back, try not to get your hopes up. If he's not making an actual effort, don't put too much effort in either because you'll end up feeling worse when the conversation doesn't go anywhere.

When guys do this, sometimes it can be because they genuinely want to know how you're doing and they want a way to open a conversation.

Most of the time, it's because they want an ego boost. (They may have sent the same message to a lot of girls.) Or, it's because they don't want you to forget about them even though they don't want to be with you.

Make sure you know which one of these scenarios you are in and be prepared for no response once you've replied so you're not left disappointed.

Remember, When your ex only gets in touch to wish you "Happy Holiday's", then he's no better than a Facebook friend. You know... someone who only messages because a reminder popped up on their phone.

If your ex is doing this to you, take a moment to assess the situation because it may be time to 'unfriend' him.

See the Facts not the Fantasy

It's normal to miss an ex.
I'm sure you had some really good times, otherwise you wouldn't be so heartbroken.

As time goes on, your memory can be a bit selective in what it remembers.

Most people tend to only think of the good things about a relationship once it has ended and seem to forget the things that they weren't happy about.

Even worse, people have a habit of idealising their ex and telling themselves stories of how great things could have been in the future by filling in the blanks with romanticised versions of their ex.

When this happens, you can start to miss them more and feel like you'll never meet anyone like them. In reality there is someone out there who will be so much better than your ex. You just have to believe it and get yourself to a place where you are ready to move on and meet someone new.

So, when you start to feel like you really miss your ex again, take a pen and paper and start listing the things you didn't like. Remember him for the real him and not the made-up version in your head.

Go Fishing When You're Ready, Not When People Tell You To

There may come a point in time when, a couple months into a breakup, you feel like you should be diving back into the 'Dating Sea'.

Or, maybe your friends are telling you that you need to get back out there and meet a new guy.

—Even though you don't feel ready yet.

If this happens, ***do not*** listen to them.

Getting over someone isn't about going out there and partying your sorrows away, or finding a new boyfriend as soon as you can.

It's about doing the things that feel right for you in order to heal and eventually feel great again. There are ways you can help yourself start the process of moving on quicker (acceptance being a great start).

There is no time limit on when that should be, regardless of what anyone else thinks.

Whenever I would ignore my own feelings and force myself to go out to a bar before I was feeling ready to, I would end up having the worst night.

Not only did it end up being a waste of makeup and money, the hangover the next day made it even less worth it.

If going out and meeting new guys isn't where you are at, listen to your heart and don't let the pressure of time or people get to you.

Unless He Has Amnesia, He Hasn't Forgotten About You

Cutting contact from your ex after a breakup is probably the best thing you could do for yourself, but let's be honest, it's not easy and it doesn't make you feel great.

When you don't hear from your ex for a while, it can feel like he's forgotten that you existed at all (completely not the case by the way).
I know what you're thinking though.
He would have gotten in touch to see how you were doing, but he hasn't, so that's definitely what's happened.

Again, not the case.

Just because you haven't heard from him doesn't mean you're not on his mind.
How many times have you thought about your ex lately but resisted the temptation to message him, even though you wanted to?

The reason I brought this point up is because, even though radio silence is necessary to help you get over your person, sometimes the irrational feeling that they have forgotten about your entire existence can feel really awful and having the reassurance that they haven't can take a bit of weight off.

So, chin up.

He hasn't forgotten you.

He's probably hurting too and wondering if he made a mistake by letting you go.

I'm sure this makes you feel better.

Just remember, unless he realises it and comes back to you, the best thing you can do is work on being happy and feeling good without him.

If You're Having Trouble Letting Go, Lock It Up

This exercise really helped me when I was struggling to let go of the hurt and disappointment of yet another failed relationship.

For this you will need the following:

1x Small box
1x Pen
1x Notepad
1x Scented Candle (not necessary, but I found it to be more relaxing)

Instructions:

1. Find a quiet space where you won't be interrupted for at least 10 minutes and light the candle.
2. Close your eyes for a few moments and allow your mind and body to relax.
3. Now, think about the things that you no longer want in your present life.
4. Using your pen and notepad, write 'Goodbye' followed by whatever it is you no longer need in your life.
5. Each time you write goodbye to what you don't want, put that piece of paper into the

box and seal it. Put it away somewhere so that you won't see it everyday.
6. Once you are finished, Say goodbye and picture those negative thoughts and energies leaving your body once and for all.

Letting go isn't always easy, even when we know it's not good for us. But this process of writing everything down on paper can also feel like you're getting it out of your system and out of your body. Being able to see your thoughts and feelings on paper will separate it from you. By physically locking it away in a box and putting it out of sight, it helps you remove it from your predominant thoughts.

Saying goodbye to your old emotions and getting rid of negative energy will help to clear your mind and allow space for new and more positive energy to come in.

Girl, Stop Feeling Sorry for Yourself!

There was a time when I had to hear this, so maybe you do too.

Shit has happened, and yes it may have been unfair and undeserved, but it has happened, nonetheless.

Nothing can be done to change it now, so if you're still moping about it and feeling sorry for yourself.

Stop it.

There are much worse things going on in the world right now than some dumb guy who can't see your worth.

Take some time today to practice some gratitude.

Think about the things you have in your life right now.

Maybe it's support from your friends, love from your family, financial security from your job, or even something as small as M&S still having your favourite sandwich.

Whatever the reason, find *something* to be grateful for.

Remove yourself from the pity party, give yourself a reality check and stop feeling sorry for yourself.

Time to Move onto Bigger Better Things

You're Not Aladdin So Stop Wishing Your Life Away While He's Getting on With His

After a breakup, it's natural to sit in the house and mope whilst wishing you and your ex were still together.
Or, call your friends in the middle of the night, crying and talking for hours about how this could have happened.

What girl hasn't been there?

However, there comes a point when enough is enough. You have to get out of bed, jump in the shower, wash your hair and start enjoying life again.

Sitting around, wishing things could be different, is about as effective as rubbing your bedside lamp and expecting a magic genie to pop out.

If you continue to waste time on scenarios of him wanting you back, instead of focusing on ways in which you can start to feel happy without him in your life, you end up slowing your own progress.

Worse still, you might find yourself still stuck in the same place months from now, whilst your ex has already moved on.

If you don't want that to happen, now is the time to stop wishing and start working on moving forward.

Time To Get Over A Breakup
≤
Length of the Relationship

This is a rule I have for myself when dealing with breakups.
When things don't work out with someone, I make a promise to never spend more time being upset over the person than the length of the relationship.

I'm not saying you have to completely get over your ex, but make sure that you're not over-investing your time dwelling on the relationship ending.

When you first break up with someone, it's natural to prioritise your thoughts on them. Everything else gets pushed to the back of the queue.
That's okay!
Just make sure that this person doesn't stay at the forefront of your mind for longer than they deserve to be there.
That's why I like to give it a time limit that lasts no longer than how long the entire relationship lasted.
Make a promise to yourself that, before this time is up, you will find something else to be the first thing you think about when you wake up in the morning.

This is where working on you comes in handy.

When you start to focus on your own happiness, you start getting busier doing the things that you love. When you do that, you change your priorities. Your ex is no longer the first thing you think about and you start to enjoy life without him.

Dwelling on something for longer than it lasted is a waste of your precious time and energy.
Don't give someone more than they deserved from you.

You already gave them your time during your relationship.
Don't waste any more on them.
It's your time now; make sure you use it on you.

Are You Psychic? Didn't Think So...

Are you torturing yourself with thoughts of what could have been? Or telling yourself that the relationship would have been perfect, If only he would give it another chance?

It's easy to let your imagination run wild and fill your head with perfectly presumed scenarios of what your future would have been like if you and your ex were still together.

But don't let these daydreams consume your mind and trick you into believing that they're a prediction of what would have happened.

Because the truth is, you just don't know.

It could have been the most romantic love story ever or it could have been a complete disaster.

Put an end to the unnecessary grieving over your imagined future.

Remind yourself that even though you may have had good times in your relationship, those good times might not have lasted.

It'll make it much easier to let go.

Remember, you are *not psychic.*

You cannot predict the future.

Hell, most of the psychics out there can't even predict the future half the time!
So there's no point in you trying to.

Spend less time thinking about the future you think you would have had and more time focussing on the future you want to have.

Look at This Loss as Making Space Instead

When a relationship is over, it can feel like you've lost everything and you're consumed with thoughts of what used to be and the sadness of what is no more.

And while you may have lost your "in a relationship" status and no longer have a boyfriend, there is another way to look at the situation.

Now that you are single again, there is space in your life for someone new and better to come along.

Trust that the universe is trying to make it happen for you.

Imagine an amazing guy, that you had an amazing connection with, came along when you were still in your relationship with your ex.
You would have missed your chance because you were with someone who turned out to be a frog rather than a prince.

Instead of looking at this as a loss and wishing you were back in a relationship, try to see it as a new opportunity to attract someone into your life who is more on your level.

If you continue to hold on to the memories of your ex and let your mind only focus on them, that space gets taken up again and there's no longer any room for anything new to move in.

It's not easy letting go, but when you do, you make room for new and exciting things to happen.

Let Go and Let the Universe Do Its Job

Sometimes, people that breakup get back together and end up living happily ever after.

It's okay if you still believe that your ex is the person you are meant to be with, even if you are separated right now.

If you feel that this person is right for you and that you should be together, then the best thing you can do is let him go.

You might be thinking, "But if he's the one for me, why do I have to let him go?"

Just because you might feel this way, doesn't mean the other person is in the same place as you. Maybe they are not ready and if that's the case, you can't make them feel ready.

That's up to them.

Have faith and don't try to force anything, because if it's truly meant to be, fate will step in and make it happen for you.

Now I'm not saying that you should sit and wait for him to come back to you just because you're sure he's the one for you.

Quite the opposite, actually.

Get out there and live your life the way you want to. Achieve the goals you want. Do the things you want and get yourself to a good place in life.

That is your only job because when you're feeling good, the universe will deliver good things to you. If this ex is good for you, then your paths will cross again.
And if not, someone new and even better will come along.

You have to let go of your ex and the idea of getting back together any time soon.

If you two are meant for each other, the Universe will make it happen for you.

You do your job and let the Universe do its job.

You're Not Going to Notice a Great Guy When You're Not Ready

If it's been a few months since your breakup and you're starting to feel the pressure to 'get back out there'. Try not to give yourself too hard a time.

If you don't feel ready to meet someone new, then you don't have to.

I know it can be difficult if you have outside influences telling you otherwise. I have been told several times from friends, family and work colleagues that I need to put myself out there as soon as possible to get over my breakup.

But the truth was that I wasn't ready yet. And just because I was feeling better about my breakup, It didn't mean that I wanted to date a new guy.

I knew that, with the way I was feeling, even if the most amazing guy came along, I wouldn't have been able to appreciate him or even see how amazing he was.

Whenever I did drag myself out when I wasn't feeling up to it, I never met anyone.

It was only when I was feeling good and when I wanted to go out and have fun again, that things started to happen.

It's true, you have to be open to love and new opportunities in love, But you also have to be ready.

The universe knows if you're not prepared for what *or who* is meant for you. Instead of feeling bad because everyone's telling you what you should be doing, take all the time you need to fully heal and get into a good headspace.

Ignore what everyone else has to say. There's no time limit on how long it should take before you start dating again.
This is your life. You get to decide when the time is right and then the universe will decide when to give you what you deserve.

Don't Stay the 'Heartbroken Girl' Because You're Afraid of What's Next

The transition from being a girl who is heartbroken to a girl who is over the breakup—but on her own—can be just as scary as going from being in a relationship to being single.

Why?

Because most people don't like change, even if it is for the better.
Change of any kind takes them out of their comfort zone.

When you are at this place in your life, it can feel like you're between worlds.

No longer the hurt girl from the past. Not quite the new girl who is following her dreams and living a happy, free, single life.

You are now transitioning from "heartbroken" to something completely new and exciting. This can feel daunting because now you have to look at yourself and really ask, ***what do you want?***

The question isn't scary.

It's the answers that we fear because it may mean there's more work to do.

If you're feeling this way, don't be afraid to step into this new version of you and figure out what you want from life now.

If not, you might find yourself stuck in limbo, between your heartbroken past and your promising future.

Things Can Change in an Instant

You may already know this if you weren't expecting your relationship to end.

But just as quickly as things can change for the worst, they can always change again for the better.

I remember when I started dating a guy I really liked. I would think back to before we met.

I was in a good place. I was happy and content. I wasn't thinking about how I was going to meet someone.

I was on a family holiday just enjoying exploring feeling grateful for the experience. I had no intention of meeting anyone in a foreign country.

Then out of the blue, he came along.

It reminded me that you really can't predict what will happen and when.

It just does.

So, if you're feeling in disbelief and shock at your breakup, just know that things can always change in an instant.

You will feel shock and disbelief again, but in a good way.

You Need Some Fresh 'Ex-Free' Air

I don't mean literally, although that does help too.

This is more of a "spring clean" of your ex. It's time to get rid of the text messages, the photos, the hoodie he wore.
Anything that is a reminder of your ex, clear it out of your current space.

If you're not ready to delete the messages or photos, archive them until you are.
If you're not quite ready to throw the hoody out, box it away so it's out of sight.
Get rid of any belongings, reminders and gifts, or at least put them in storage so you're not always looking at them.

It also helps to do a full clearcut and get rid of anything you no longer need or use.

Think of it the same way you open your window to get stale air out and let fresh air in.
Give your phone and your personal space a fresh start and make room for newness to come in.

When I get to this stage, I like to do a full wardrobe clear out and get rid of anything that I no longer use.

Once I'm done, I feel so much better and I get the best sleep that night.

Remember, everything is made up of energy—even clothes and objects.
If you're still wearing your ex's hoodie, it's made up of energy too.

Get rid of stale, past energy that resides in your ex's belongings and anything else you have.
The constant reminders and wasted space are no good to you.

Clear it all out and let some fresh air and new opportunities into your life.

When You Get to Look Back and Wonder, "What Was I Thinking?"

Seriously though... what were you thinking?

Let's be honest, we've all been here with at least one ex. It's such a freeing feeling knowing that you no longer want him back.

Even better when you've realised that he was so wrong for you.

When you get to this stage, take a moment to reflect on how far you've come.
Remember the time when you thought you would never stop crying and never get over the heartbreak?

Well you're here now, so give yourself a pat on the back!

Be proud that you have been able to come this far and take a moment to feel how amazing it is to get to this stage. I'm sure at some point you never thought you would.

Know that you have grown and that all the things you have learned through the process are going to take you to even better things.

This is the perfect time to start thinking about what you want and putting it out into the universe.

Whether it's new love, a new career, or even a change in lifestyle that you want, write it all down. Once you're finished, you can start to make plans on how to achieve them.

If you aren't at this stage yet, don't worry, you will get there. And when you do, celebrate it because it's a great achievement!

Don't Be Bitter, Be Better

When you get to the point where you are pretty much over your ex, or you at least know that you don't want him back anymore, It can feel amazing knowing how far you've come.

However, even though you know now that this person was not right for you, Make sure that you're not holding on to any resentment or bitterness from how they treated you.

Because that can still affect you going forward.

When you talk about your ex now, and the things he did, Are your words spoken with calmness or is there spite and anger in your voice?

Because if there is, a part of you is still holding on to the past.

When you continue to allow these thoughts to make you feel angry in the present, you cause yourself to relive the pain that you went through.

As hard as it may be, try to find a way to fully accept that what is done is done.

The past can't be changed so there is no point in feeling bitter about it.

Learning to accept what happened to you, and not letting that thought affect you today, is the key to growth and becoming a better version of yourself.

Yes, your ex may have been an absolute a**hole.

But remember, he is no longer your problem.

Don't let the memories of him rile you up and leave a bitter taste in your mouth.

Don't Get Stuck in Love Limbo

Why is it that some people get chatted up more than others when they are out?

It's not all to do with how they look or dress. It's also about the energy that they put out. I've been told in the past that when I'm out at a bar I put out a vibe that I'm not single or that I don't want to be approached. I was initially surprised by this, and argued that whenever I'm out I am usually smiling and laughing. (I definitely don't suit the whole pouty, moody/sexy look.) My friend explained to me that I was solely focused on my friends, that I completely closed myself off to anyone outside my circle.

You may find this contradicts the whole, "If you don't look for it, that's when it will happen" theory. I'm not saying you should go 'right-swipe crazy' on Tinder or chat up every guy who comes into your orbit on a night out. I just mean be open to the possibility of someone new coming into your life.

The vibe/energy that we emit comes back to us.

If you're sending out signals that you are unavailable, It will subconsciously be picked up by the people around you.

Head into a night out with an open mind and an open heart; send that open energy out and let the universe do the rest.

It's okay to give yourself time to heal after a breakup. In fact, it is necessary.
Just be careful that you don't close yourself off fully to the idea of someone new coming into your life. It's completely understandable to be a bit fearful to get into another relationship or even start dating again when you've gone through a bad breakup. I was single for almost a year before I got back out there.

If you let yourself get too comfortable in the 'in-between' stage, you could end up giving off the wrong vibes and close yourself off to new opportunities without realising it.

Remember Who You Were

There was a time before all of this heartache.

A time before you even knew your ex existed, and before your happiness relied on someone else's actions.

It's that moment when you are single and not in like or love with someone. That's when you are at your most confident and free.

This is because you don't have anyone occupying your mind and affecting your emotions. You have more time to think about your own needs and do the things that make you happy.
I always find that once I'm at the point where I'm not wanting or missing someone who is no longer in my life, I revert back to who I was before I met that person.

That's when I'm most empowered.

I feel carefree. I can do anything I want. I'm always excited for what's to come.
And when I'm feeling good, that's when good things happen.

I'm not saying that having someone isn't a good thing, but if things do turn out for the worst, it's time to remember the person you were and get her back.

Once you start to feel like you again, you'll start to remember how amazing you really are, how capable you are, and you'll remember that you can do, be, and have anything you want.
Remember what it's like to feel independent and free. Remember that you were happy before your ex and that will give you comfort in knowing you're going to be happy after him too.

Remember how amazing you were and go get that girl back!

Let Today Be Friend Appreciation Day!

Okay, so you've probably been through a lot in the last few months, but I'm sure you've not been through it alone.

Take today to give thanks to the friends who:

- Had your best interests at heart.
- Were always there when you needed them.
- Made you laugh when you were feeling sad.
- Messaged you every day to make sure you were okay.
- Believed in you, even when you didn't believe in yourself.
- Listened to you for hours and felt your pain as if it were theirs.
- Stayed up late on the phone with you while you cried your heart out.
- Dropped everything to visit you when you had a bad day.

- Drove straight over to see how you were doing right after your breakup.

- Brought you wine and pizza, so you weren't hungry and feeling alone.

- Listed all the reasons why your ex was a loser—even if he wasn't really that bad.

- Dragged you out and got you good and drunk to forget your sorrows for one night.

Let's be honest, you probably wouldn't have gotten this far without them.

I know I wouldn't have.

So make their day and let them know how much they mean to you.

Self-Worth Work

It's All About You Now!

The Universe Knows When It's Not Your Time

I believe the universe brings us challenging circumstances so that we can learn lessons and grow within ourselves.

I also find that if we don't learn the lessons the first time around, the universe throws us more obstacles to face until we do.

If you find that you always end up stuck in the same situations when it comes to relationships, or even life in general, ask yourself what you have learned from the experience.

Think about the things that have happened and whether or not you could have dealt with the situation better. Be honest with yourself about whether you need to work more on *you*.
As you can probably tell from my experiences, I have not had the best of luck with relationships. Now, I can confidently say that I am not a bad person and I believe that I deserve a loving, happy relationship just as much as anyone else.

But after a few heartbreaks, I had to ask myself, "Do I need to change?"

The answer was yes. But not in the way you might think. It wasn't my hair, clothes, job or waistline that I had to change.

It was my self-worth.

I needed time to work on healing the wounds of my inner child and work on loving myself again. Once I did, I was able to see where I could have done things differently in my past relationships and also understood why they didn't work out.
This healing completely changed my outlook on life and made me understand what I really wanted and made me so grateful none of the past ones worked out.
If they had, I would never have worked on my own healing and become who I am today.

If you find yourself asking why your relationships aren't working out, it could be because you still haven't learned what you're meant to.

Until you do, the universe won't give you what you want because you're not ready for it yet.

Learn To Love Yourself Before You Love Again

The ending of a relationship can leave emotional wounds that, if not addressed, can cause problems in future relationships.

For example, if you were cheated on by someone, this can leave feelings of insecurity—feeling like you are not good enough.

If these emotions are not realised and dealt with, they can resurface in a new relationship which can be identified by certain actions.

You might be paranoid that your new person is going to cheat on you. You constantly need reassurance. You develop controlling tendencies and self sabotage ("I might as well mess things up now, because I'm bound to at some point").

Not only can these things ruin your new relationship, but in a sense your new partner is being punished for things you carry from your previous one.

Don't let your ex continue to affect you long after he is gone.

If you have been hurt or disappointed in the past, don't look to a new relationship to heal you. Only you can heal yourself.

Take a good look at who you are and how you are feeling about yourself.

Do you feel worthy and deserving?
Do you feel confident and self assured?
Do you feel like you are emotionally able to accept what you deserve and reject what you don't?

If the answer is no, then find ways to get yourself there.

Whether it's through therapy, self help books or advice from friends and family, invest some time and love on yourself and you'll come out stronger and more prepared for happiness.

Who Said Being Single Was a Bad Thing?

When someone asks if you are single and then proceeds with, "Don't worry, you'll meet someone soon".

Just say, "Oh I know, I'm not worried at all. I'm just taking my time, making sure I pick a good one".

Do not let people feel sorry for you because you are single.

Being single doesn't mean you are not good enough, that you are alone or unhappy.

Take pride in knowing that you aren't rushing straight into a new relationship and that you are capable of being on your own.

So many people aren't. They let the fear of being on their own cause them to settle for anyone who's available at the time.

It's okay to take your time deciding who you want to give your time to and what you want your next relationship to be like. The more time you spend, the better your chance of meeting Mr Right, not Mr Right Now.

Even more to the point, If you actually want to stay single for a bit and take some time out for yourself to travel, work on your career, soul search, etc.

That's okay too!

Don't let people throw you a pity party that you have no intention of attending.

There are worse things than being single!

—Even if others don't think so.

Believe You Are Worthy of More and You Will Get More

They say that people will only treat you the way you let them. While this is true, it's also easier said than done.

Just knowing that you don't deserve to be treated poorly will not stop it from happening.

You have to truly know that you deserve better and take appropriate action to reflect that.

How many times have friends told you that the person you're dating isn't deserving of you?
Or how many times have you told yourself they shouldn't treat you the way they do, but you still have them around?

It's insecurity and uncertainty within ourselves that causes us to allow toxic people to mistreat us.

This stops us from walking away when, deep down, we know we should.

You see, just being aware that someone isn't treating you right isn't enough to make you let them go.

You have to be at a point where you are so secure in who you are and what you want, that you will discard and walk away from anything that doesn't resemble it without a second thought.

Believe deep down that you are worthy of more.

When you do, that's when you will start to rid yourself of the people who contradict those beliefs.

Become the Queen of Confidence

Have you ever looked at a girl and thought to yourself, "I wish I had her confidence"?
Well you can. You just have to "fake it 'til you make it".

This is a little exercise that I learned from a young age as a shy and unconfident girl.

I would picture a version of me that was confident. I would imagine the ways I would walk, talk, and how I would act if I was someone who was self-assured.

Then every day, I would try to be that girl as best I could. Then one day, I realised that I had become her.

If you feel like you've lost some confidence during this breakup or you just need a little boost, I suggest adding this to your routine.

In the morning, while you are having your cup of tea or coffee, sit and picture how you would like your day to go, and more importantly, a new more confident version of you.

Imagine in your mind how you would feel, what you would say to the people you came across throughout your day, and how you would handle different situations that came your way.

Once you have this version of you in your mind, remember it for the rest of the day and before you do or say something, ask yourself, what would the *confident* me do?

Then go and do it.

It will feel a little strange at first, but the more you get into that habit, the more you will push through your limits and do things you never thought you could.

Before you know it, people will be telling you how much they wish they had your confidence.

Then, you can pass on the secret.

Remember this, if you want to be treated like a queen: you have to act like one.

Don't Try to Be Perfect, No One Really Wants That

Think about the people you have dated in the past; think about your favourite things about them.

What comes to mind?

I am willing to bet that the things that you thought about weren't much to do with how 'perfect' they were at everything.

I imagine you would have been attracted to things like their hair when it was all messy, the way they pronounced a certain word, when they got nervous over silly things, their weird food combos, or even their obsession with birds.

Whatever qualities you liked, I bet it was the quirky and unique ones that made you like that person even more.

What I'm trying to say is don't stress yourself out trying to be the 'perfect girl'.

No one's really looking for that.

It is your cute and distinctive traits that someone falls in love with.

If you meet a guy who is expecting perfection or feels the need to point out your 'flaws' then he's not the one for you.

Find a man who loves you because of your imperfections and not in spite of them.

You Are Magic, Not Mediocre

Any guy who makes you feel like you are average and nothing special is not deserving of you. The way someone treats you is usually a reflection on how they feel about themselves; they are trying to bring you to their level.

When you let someone make you feel like you are not good enough, you are giving them the power to affect you.

That power should only belong to you.

Whenever this happens, dissociate from the situation and look at it logically.
It will help you see this guy for who they really are without any emotional bias.

When you take your feelings out of the equation, you might realise that this guy's actions are proving that he's not so great, or at least he's not good enough for you and what you need.

Realise that you can take back control by changing how you view a situation, even if you can't change the person in the situation.

Don't let anyone try to take that power away from you and control you.

Remember how magical and special you are!

"I Bet You're Missing Me Now"

Can you imagine the type of person who would say this to an ex?

I think of someone strong and independent—confident that they are worth missing.

I love this bad-ass energy and the feeling it brings.

When you go through a breakup, your self-esteem can take a bit of a hit.
Feelings of rejection can make you feel like you are not worthy.
Confidence is lost and you end up thinking you are not good enough.

While it may be natural to feel this way, know that these feelings are no reflection on who you really are.

Find ways to regain your confidence and work on getting yourself to the point where you feel so good that anytime your ex pops into your head, you think, "I bet you're missing me now!"

Focus on embodying this bad-ass energy and being the superwoman that you are.

Although you may not be feeling amazing right now, Use this breakup as an opportunity to grow and transform into an even better version of you.

Make a change and do something that empowers you.

You can do *anything* you want!

Do the things that make you feel empowered because you will get over this and he will end up missing you.

Don't forget, there's a bad-ass in every one of us. It's time to release it and show him exactly what you're made of.

"Yeah, I Have High Standards. What's Your Point?"

I used to think that I couldn't be kind and compassionate, as well as bold and badass.
My kindness knew no boundaries and I'd end up lowering my standards as a result.

Have you ever felt like you couldn't speak up about something because you didn't want to seem too demanding, even though you weren't happy in a situation?

This is partly because whenever women try to voice their feelings, they have been labelled with terms such as "crazy", "too opinionated", "too demanding", "too clingy" etc.
It's made us afraid to say how we really feel, causing us to suffer in silence just to keep the peace.

Don't let anyone mistake your kindness for weakness. Standing up for yourself and asking for your needs to be met does not mean you're being difficult, high maintenance or a bitch.

It means you respect yourself enough to fight for what you want and strong enough to dismiss what you don't.

Don't ever lower your standards for anyone because you'll never be satisfied.

Just because we should all practice more kindness doesn't mean we can't be confident and empowering too.

You can be both, so don't be afraid to let your inner bad-ass out when it's called for.

Make a Vision Board

It's time to put the focus back on you! When you've come through the toughest part of a breakup, It can leave you feeling somewhat lost.

Going through a breakup can be such a life changing event. It definitely forces us to grow in ways we never intended.

This is the perfect time for you to re-evaluate what you want from your life and decide how you want to live it going forward.

Your main goal then was to try and get through it one day at a time. But now you are feeling more like yourself again, it can be a great time to refocus your goals and start going for them.

Think about what you really want from life. Not your 'achievable goals', but the ones you think are harder to have.

Those are the ones you should go for.

I can't think of a better way to help you get focussed. Vision boards are great because they really force you to think about what you really want. They are a great daily reminder of what you're working towards and they're a lot of fun to do too!

Here's how I do it:

1. Write a list of the things I want to achieve and the images that will represent these goals. (I also like to have sections like career, lifestyle, love, health and travel.)

2. Google the images and save them to a desktop folder.

3. Using a Pages document (or the equivalent), drag the images onto the page and adjust to desired size. (I like to keep my images grouped in their sections.)

4. Add affirmations that make you feel positive, motivated and inspired.

5. Save to your desktop or print it out and place it in a place where you will see it everyday.

Getting Back Out There

What You Should Know

When You're Not Ready to Love Again Just Learn to Like Again

After a breakup, the thought of falling in love with someone new all over again can be daunting.

Don't beat yourself up if you've not got that loving feeling yet.

Just take it one step at a time.

Rather than putting pressure on the need to feel ready to love again, take a small baby-step forward and just try to feel ready to like someone new instead.

You never know, *like* can always turn into *love* very easily. Unless every one of your exes was "love at first sight" you might find that you get back into the swing of things a lot quicker than expected.

Remember, baby steps still take you places and no one is timing you but you.

If You Fear Falling, You'll Never Fly

Reaching the point where you no longer want your ex back, and realising they weren't right for you, can be an amazing feeling.

It can also feel a bit scary because for the last few months your focus has been getting over the heartbreak. When you no longer feel hurt and sad, it can leave you wondering, "What now?"

You may be feeling like you don't want to meet someone new or fall in love anytime soon because of the heartbreak you've just been through.

There's no rule book saying that once you are over someone you have to get back out there right away; you can take as much time as you need to.

However, don't let your fear or having been hurt hold you back from falling in love again.

If you don't let anyone new into your life you may prevent your heart from getting broken, but you'll also prevent any chance of you finding the love of a lifetime.

Not every relationship will end in heartbreak, but if you're afraid of opening your heart again, you'll never find out what amazing experiences the universe has in store for you.

I got to this stage at one point and it was frustrating because I didn't want to be alone forever, but I also was too afraid to step back out in the dating world.

It wasn't until one day I realised that by being fearful of getting my heart broken again, that the memory of my experiences with my ex were still affecting my life.
What this meant to me was that I was still allowing him to affect my actions in the present moment, despite me not wanting anything to do with him.

This realisation gave me a bit of a wakeup call. It made me determined not to let my fear and him stop me from moving on. He had already wasted so much of my time, I wasn't going to let him waste any more.

Love like you have never been hurt, trust like you've never been lied to, and don't let the memory of that ex you no longer want weigh you down and stop you from flying.

You Will Meet Someone New

Right now you might be thinking that you'll never meet another guy like your ex again.
I know how tough it can be, Especially if you thought this guy was your 'Mr Right'.

But the reality is that 'Mr Right' won't break your heart.

After each relationship ended, I believed that I would never meet someone that I would like as much as my ex.

And after each new relationship began, I was reminded of how wrong I was.

If you got over the last guy you dated and managed to meet this ex, you can get over this ex too and meet someone else.

Even though you don't believe it right now, trust me when I say that someone new will come along.

You will be happy again.

And you will forget all about this ex, just like you forgot about the last one.

You Can't Force What's Not Meant to Be

How dreamy would it be for your soulmate to come knocking on your door?
You probably have more chances of Tom Hardy showing up at your house.

But that doesn't mean you should canvas all the houses in your neighbourhood to find him.
Sure, you can join all the dating apps and head out to town every weekend. Theoretically, it would increase your chances of meeting someone.

But increasing your chances can still leave you nowhere.

I used to go out every weekend. Joined Tinder. Went to the gym. I did a lot of the things that people do to meet new people.

Incredibly, I had zero luck at meeting anyone.

I know what you're thinking. Maybe I came off too desperate—I promise I didn't.

But for some reason, I just didn't meet anyone that I liked enough to give out my number, let alone date.

It always seemed to happen for me when I least expected it. Those were the ones that turned out to be something more.

Have you ever dated someone and then, after talking for a while, you find that you always went to the same night club every weekend, but you both couldn't understand how you never noticed each other.

That is because things happen when and where they are supposed to happen.

If you're being proactive and doing all the things your previous single friends did and you're still having no luck, take a break from it and work on trusting the universe to make things happen for you.

As much as you shouldn't sit in and wait for prince charming to come knocking, forcing it won't help either.

Meaningless Company Can Be Just as Lonely

They say that the best way to get over someone is to get under someone new.

But that's only true when the new person is someone you actually like.

It's natural to feel lonely after a breakup and miss someone you most likely spent every day with, ate dinner with, and woke up next to every day.

If you go searching for intimacy and connection with any random person that's available, you'll end up settling and you might end up feeling worse afterwards.

If it is just sex you're after, then who am I to judge?

However, if what you're really missing is intimacy, I promise you won't find it in a one-night stand. And if you do, that feeling will be gone when they are and you might be left feeling empty and icky afterwards.

So, if you're spending your time with someone new, make sure it's for reasons that work for you and your needs.

Be the Kind of Person You Want to Be With

Do you want to meet someone who is kind, compassionate, understanding, ambitious, successful, strong, independent or confident?

Who doesn't!

But are you also kind, compassionate, understanding, ambitious, successful, etc.?

If you're not all these things, then the chances of you attracting them are pretty slim.

I mean, you might meet him, but your energies won't match and there's a good chance that it won't work out.

Like attracts like. Whatever energy you are putting out is going to come back to you.

You can't expect someone to bring all these great qualities to a relationship if you are not also able to bring them.

It's okay to have high standards and to want to meet an amazing person.

Just remember that an amazing person is also going to want to be with someone amazing.

If right now you are hoping to meet someone who has the best qualities, make sure you also have the best qualities for them.

If you don't, then get to work on becoming the type of person you want to be with.

Level Up!

I've had more than my fair share of unsuccessful relationships. And after each one "KO'd" It felt like another big blow to my heart.

I felt like I was cursed with bad luck in love, playing in a game I would never win.

Each time I lost, I thought it was game over and that I would never find the right guy.

But the truth is, the game was never over. There was always a different experience or someone new to make me realise why the last guy wasn't right for me.

Imagine your breakups are like a game of Mortal Kombat.

Treat each breakup like passing a level in the game. Pass enough levels and eventually you'll win.

As hard as breakups are, you can always take something from them.
Whether it's knowledge about what you would do differently, finding out something new about yourself, or figuring out what you don't want, there are always lessons you can learn.

It took me a long time to figure out who I was and what I really wanted from life.
If I didn't go through both good and bad experiences, I probably wouldn't have figured it out. I became grateful for the bad experiences because of how they shaped me into the person I am today.
As tough a time as you're having, just remember, with every breakup, you are levelling up in the process and eventually, you will reach the top.

Don't Let Society Make You Feel Guilty Because You Refuse to Settle

When you're on your own and everyone around you seems to be happily settled down, It can feel somewhat unsettling.

So many questions can run through your mind. Questions like:

Why haven't I met the right person?
What's wrong with me?"
Why do things never work out the way I want?
Are they right, am I too fussy?

Don't listen to these negative thoughts. They will do you no good.

I know it can be difficult, with social media platforms like Instagram showing off these perfect 'couple goals' lifestyles and even pressure from friends and family to meet someone.

But do it in your own time and in your own way.

For a start, most of these instagram posts aren't even a depiction of real life and your friends and family only want the best for you. They probably don't mean to put pressure on you.

Don't let these outside influences cause you to settle or lower your standards because you deserve to have the relationship you want. You don't need to settle for whatever is available just now.
Take your time. Have faith that the relationship you deserve is coming to you and
don't settle just for the sake of it.

You'll never be happy if you do.

It Only Takes One

If you're feeling a bit down about being single and thinking that you'll never meet the right person for you, remember this:

It only takes one.

One chance. One moment. One meeting. One interaction. One hello.

One person to change everything.

There are billions of people in the world and you only need to meet *one*.

While it's true that not everyone you meet will be right for you, know that there is at least one person that is.

And, you can meet him at any given time or place.

When the time is right, he will cross your path.

So, don't give up because you never know what's just around the corner.

There Are Good Things About Being Single

Now, I'm not saying that you will be single forever, but take this time to enjoy the benefits of being single. You never know, you might not want a boyfriend after seeing this.

- Your time is all yours.
- It's all about you, practice self love.
- You don't have anyone to answer to.
- Dinner is whatever you want it to be.
- You can rest, knowing that you didn't settle.
- You can do what you want, when you want.
- You don't have to shave your legs every other day.
- The excitement of the unknown, anything can happen.
- You can get your flirt on (who doesn't love a bit of flirting).
- You get the whole bed to yourself–and no more snoring.
- You no longer have to put up with the things that annoyed you about your ex.
- You now have the opportunity to find someone who doesn't have the annoying qualities your ex did.
- You can binge-watch a full Netflix show and you don't have to wait for anyone else to watch it with you.

- You can take as long as you want to get ready and you won't have anyone moaning at you to hurry up.
- The grass isn't always greener on the other side. How many friends have said that relationships aren't what they're cracked up to be?

Believe in Divine Timing

If you're finding that nothing new seems to be happening in your life right now, and nothing is the way you want, try to remember that there could be a reason why. And have faith that things will work out for you in the end.

I remember when I signed my contract to publish my first book. I was advised that it may be a couple of months before I would hear anything and that my manuscript was in a queue waiting to be read. I was fine with this at first. However, after four months had passed and I still hadn't heard anything, I began to get impatient.

I started worrying that my time was being wasted and I became annoyed at the thought that if I had went with a different publisher, I would have had my book out by now.
After several emails and calls to my publisher, I was still no further forward.

My book was basically still in the queue.
There was nothing I could do but let it go and trust that it would happen sooner than later.

Fast forward a few more months and the UK went into a national lockdown.
I was no longer able to work.

This was a really tough time for me in the beginning. Not only because I like to keep busy but because I was stuck in the house with my family every day, and as much as I love them, it was not an easy time!
Let's just say, I knew my hypnotherapist's phone number by heart by the end of lockdown.

The first week of lockdown ended with me in tears and wondering how I was going to cope for the next few months. My mental health took a major dive. Miraculously enough, two days after my mini breakdown, my proofs arrived!

They could not have come at a better time!

I was so grateful because the distraction was exactly what I needed to help get me through the mental struggles of lockdown – they literally saved me.

Whenever I find myself questioning where the thing I want is, I remind myself of this story. I honestly believe that divine timing was at play here and it protected me from months of feeling stuck and useless.

If you're still wondering why you haven't meant someone yet or why your life isn't as fabulous as you'd like yet, remember this story or think of one of your own and start to believe in divine timing.

When the time is right for you, the things you want will start to flow to you.

It Can Happen Any Time and Any Place

Are you wondering when and where you're going to meet someone?
Don't.
It can literally happen at any moment.

If you're actively going out and trying new things and still haven't met anyone, don't think that it is hopeless.
I'll be honest, I actually never had much luck meeting guys when I was making a conscious effort to. It just never happened.
In fact, I seemed to have worse luck when I tried.

So I stopped trying.

I let go and went with the flow instead.

Then boom!

That was when it happened, out of the blue and unexpected.

I've met guys at the gym, on holiday, at weddings, in coffee shops, and even just walking down the street. I can honestly say before each meeting I had, I never woke up that morning thinking, I want to meet someone today.

What I'm trying to say is that anything can happen at any time. Some things just can't be planned, so don't worry about how you're going to meet a new guy.
Because you'll never guess it right.

I'm not saying that this will happen for you in the exact same way. But if you're like me, you don't have much luck when you try to go out and meet new people.

Maybe, don't try.

Just go out and do your own thing and who knows, you might just end up in the right place at the right time.

Dating Tips

It's Always Good to Be Prepared!

Spend More Time Choosing a Man Than You Would a Designer Handbag

Imagine you decide to buy a designer handbag.

Do you go for the first one you see?

Or, do you take your time researching, looking at different styles, outweighing the pros and cons and only buying it once you are sure you've made the right choice?

Most people will take their time when making a big investment.

It's the smart thing to do.

If you can spend that much time deciding on a bag, I think it's okay to spend a little more time deciding on what type of person you want to be with.

Like you would a bag, take your time to get to know the person you are dating.

Do they treat you well?
Do they make you laugh?
Are you really compatible?
Do they share your values in life?

Make sure that the pros outweigh the cons.

You're deciding on who you're going to give your time—and eventually your heart—to.

If you can spend time deciding what type of bag to have hanging off your arm, you can spend a little more deciding what type of person you want in your arms.

How to Spot a F**KBoy

1. He thinks it is acceptable to send you pictures of his privates and is even offended when you don't go rushing to him. A guy who feels the need to do this clearly has no chat. And believe me when I say, that picture has probably been sent to every girl in his phonebook.

2. You chat every day, and even sometimes on the phone, but he's never tried to make arrangements to meet you. Unless he works away for long periods of time, this guy either gets enough of an ego boost from just chatting to you, he doesn't feel the need to meet you, or he's dating other girls and you're a backup in case it doesn't work out with the others.

3. He wants your first date to be at his house. This is not only cost-effective for him, but requires minimal effort. Give your time to a guy who is actually willing to go out of his way to meet you rather than one who expects you to come knocking on his door.

4. You had a good first date but now he's fallen off the radar. You didn't put out right away so he's moved on to the next. He will be back though, when he's been rejected elsewhere, but you can choose to ignore his texts.

5. He'll message you and then when you reply, he doesn't message back until a few days later. His, no doubt, generic text was sent to a group of girls he has stored in his phone and he's already getting his ego massaged by the girl who texted back first.

6. When he pays you backhanded compliments like, "You look nice when you've done your makeup" or "you're actually funnier/smarter/nicer than I thought". These guys are insecure and feel the need to bring you down to feel better about themselves. Steer clear of these master manipulators. You are so much better than them and they know it.

7. Their words don't match their actions. If what they do contradicts what they said they are like, there is a good chance you're being played and this guy is trying to tell you what he thinks you want to hear.

8. They are too intense right away. If they start planning trips away with you and talking about you meeting their parents before you've even been on a date there's a good chance they are full of it. This guy is trying to paint you an image of him being this great guy because of all the stuff they say they are going to do without having to actually do it. Believe it when you see it, babe.

9. You've been chatting for a while but it only consists of day-to-day generic chat. They don't actually ask you anything about you. This guy isn't that interested. Think about the things you would like to know about someone you liked. Would you only want to know how they are and what they are up to?

If You Have to Fight for a Man's Attention, He'll Never Be Yours

There are over *seven billion* people in the world!

Don't waste your time and effort on one who isn't acting interested enough to make an effort.
It's so typical when the guy you don't like won't leave you alone but the one you do like won't give you the time of day.

It's true. People want what they can't have. But it's a fact, not a rule.

So if there's someone you like but they're not 'feeling it', don't take that as a sign to want and chase them more.

Walk away.

Leave them be and focus on finding someone that you'll like better than them.

You *will* find them and the added bonus is that they'll also like you back.

Don't waste your time longing for someone who doesn't feel the same just because your pride and ego say so.

You'll feel so much more joy when you meet someone who reciprocates your feelings and puts in as much effort as you do.

The Right Guy at the Wrong Time Is Still the Wrong Guy

It's so frustrating when you meet a great guy for you, but the timing is not right.

Whether it's because he has to focus on his career, he's just out of a relationship, or he's just not ready to commit yet, he's telling you he can see a future with you *one day*. Then you've met the right guy at the wrong time, right?

WRONG!

If he really was the right guy for you, timing wouldn't matter.

When you meet the right person, things should just flow and it shouldn't be complicated, especially if it's a new relationship.

Now, I'm not saying that you definitely won't end up with this guy in the future.

Anything can happen.

If right now this person is not right for you, they're not in the same head space.

Maybe they have to work on themselves more or they need a little time to figure out what they want. Whatever the reason, know that when the right person comes along, timing won't be an issue.
The right guy won't need to put your relationship on pause and leave you hanging until he decides what he wants.
The only thing you can do is let him be and concentrate on your own goals.

It's hard not to want to wait for him.

But if it's truly meant to be, you will meet him again in the right place, at the right time.

And nothing will get in the way of you two being together.

Soulmates Don't Make You Feel Like Shit

Have you ever met someone who you thought was your soulmate, but things didn't work out and you were devastated because you thought that they were the one?

Well, the hard truth of the matter is that if this person was truly who you were meant to be with, then they would be with you.

If you meet your soulmate, the relationship should progress easily and naturally.

Love doesn't have to be complicated.

Don't mistake a good connection for a soulmate connection.

It's simple but true.

Your soulmate will not make you feel like shit.

When you meet the right person, they will do what it takes to be with you.

No obstacle will be too big, no distance will be too far and no situation will be solution-less.

People who love each other and want to be together will find a way to make it happen—no matter what the odds are.

If you've met someone who isn't doing these things, there's probably someone else way better out there.

Find Someone Who's There for the Good, the Bad and the 'Ugly' You

Who wouldn't want to be there for all the fun times?

Everything is always great when things are going well. The real test is when they're not.

When you're choosing a partner you want to share your life with, find someone who'll be there for you through the tough times too.

Be with someone who still wants to see you when you're having a bad day, Who tries to cheer you up when you're upset, and who doesn't walk away or go silent when you are both arguing, but sticks around to try and sort it out instead.
Find someone who thinks you're beautiful when you feel your 'ugliest' (you know what I'm talking about, hair scraped back, zero makeup, old sweatpants).

That's the person that's worth giving your time to.

The one who doesn't just want you for how you look or what you do, but who loves you because of who you are.

You deserve someone who is committed to you 100% of the time, not just for the good times.

So when you decide to commit to someone new, make sure that they want all of you, all of the time.

—Even when you're not looking or feeling your best.

Words With No Action Are Like a Phone With No Battery

They are both pretty useless.

If you've met someone who's been saying all the right things, but has yet to take any action, you might be waiting awhile.

Don't fall into the trap of liking someone for the type of person they claim to be if they haven't actually done anything to show they are who they say they are.

Watch out for people who talk a lot about all the things they want to do with you but never actually end up doing.

A guy might say to you that he wants you to go on a trip together. You could get a hotel, champagne and see the sights. He might sound genuine and go into detail about it so you think it will happen. You end up getting excited about the trip and think about how sweet this guy is.

But what if the trip never happens and it seems all forgotten about? There's a good chance he's just said it for effect rather than because he wants to go away with you.

Don't give a man credit where credit isn't due.

If words aren't followed by action, they are nothing more than empty air.

If You're Confused About Where You Stand, You've Got Your Answer

When you start dating again, it can be exciting but nerve-racking at the same time. There are so many questions going through your mind.

Are we exclusive?
Where is this going?
Does he really like me?
Is he seeing other girls?
How does he feel about me?

It's natural to feel this at the start.

But if it's been a while now and you're still wondering the same questions, you might already have your answer.

When you start dating someone and it's going well, the relationship will progress easily and naturally. There will be a mutual understanding of how you feel about each other as well as an idea of what direction the relationship is going in.
If after a few months, you're still questioning the relationship and your person isn't giving you a straight answer, then take that as their answer.

Then take that as their answer.
Guys are smarter than they let on (sometimes).

If he really wants to be with you he *will* tell you.

If you're still at the casual stage and you don't want to be, but he's not budging, it'll be because a part of him doesn't want to.

The question you need to ask yourself is, are you willing to accept this?

Relationships shouldn't be that complicated.. If you are more confused than you are content, it might be time to reevaluate your situation.

You Deserve a Guy Who Is More Afraid of Losing You Than He Is of Commitment

It's such a cliche nowadays. Guys are afraid of commitment because this one time, they got their heart broken by some girl, and they don't want to get hurt, which is why they can't commit, blah, blah, blah.

Sorry boys, you need to build a bridge and get over it.

When you meet a guy you like, who isn't ready for commitment with you, make sure you don't waste your time committing to him.

The reality is that if a guy likes you enough, he *will* commit.

Any other reason is just an excuse because they are not 100% sure of you.

Value yourself enough to know that you deserve someone who will do anything to be with you and not someone you have to convince to be with you.

So many girls out there are settling for love situations that are less than what they want—all because the guy they like isn't ready yet.

If you let a guy think that it's okay for him to be with you and not commit to you, he never will.

Don't be that girl; you're worth so much more.

A smart man will know how lucky he is to be with you and he will do anything to be with you. He will even find a way to get over his so-called, "commitment issues".

Do You Want the Good News or the Bad News First?

I usually like to hear the bad news first because then things can end on a good note. So that's where I'm going to start.

The bad news is that you can't make someone like, love, or want to be with you.

Nor can you force them to understand your point of view or see you in the way you want them to.

This is out of your control. Only they can make that decision.

The good news is that you are in control of *your own life* and can decide to not let what someone else thinks of you affect you.

When you like someone who doesn't like you back, it's natural to feel hurt and believe you're not good enough.

But think about the times when someone has liked you but you haven't felt the same.

Did you think any less of them as a person?

Or was it just that it wasn't a right fit?

You can't help who you like, love, or want. So, don't feel disheartened when it's the other way around.

When you can learn not to take rejection so personally, you'll find that it won't matter so much when your feelings aren't reciprocated.

Then you can move on to the next potential.

Chase Dreams, Not People

If you feel the urge to chase someone because you want something to happen, don't do it.
It's normal after the end of a relationship to want that feeling again and want that special someone in your life.
However, you should never feel like you need to fight for someone's attention. If they're not giving it to you freely, then they're not right for you.

Don't try and force it because it'll never happen the way you want and you can end up pushing them further away.
The more you chase this person, the less likely they are to come towards you.

Have you ever met someone who seemed lovely and had all these great qualities, but they tried too hard and no matter how much you wanted to, you just didn't feel the same?

I used to get the 'icky' feeling when this happened to me. No matter how amazing the guy seemed, I just couldn't shake the feeling.

If you know what I'm talking about then I'm sure you don't want to unintentionally give someone else the icky feeling.

This is where energy comes in.
People can sense energy, even if they don't understand it.
Whenever you try to chase someone, you are telling the universe that you don't have them, creating an energy of lack. The universe takes note of this and gives you more experiences that will make you feel needier and make you feel even more of this lack.

In order to shift this energy, let go of this person and stop chasing them because it's your best chance of getting them.
When you release that need, they will feel it. And if they want you, they will come towards you.

Focus on your goals and on becoming the best version of you. When you do, you'll attract the best toward you. Trust that the right things will happen for you when they're supposed to.
Relationships shouldn't feel like work and the only thing you should ever be chasing is your dreams. Work on the goals that will give you the life you want because when you feel good, you will attract good people to you.

Your Time Will Come

It can be frustrating and upsetting when you feel like everyone around you seems to be doing what they are supposed to with the people they are meant to be with.

Some people settle down and have kids earlier than others and if you're one of the last ones left, it can really suck!

But there could be a reason why you haven't found the relationship or partner you want yet.

It could be that the person you are meant to with hasn't become the man you deserve yet, and the universe is biding its time. It's giving you 'so so' relationships, so that you don't settle with the wrong person.

Or maybe it is you that has some work to do before you get to settle down with the right partner.

Think about the stories you hear about people who go through a shocking and terrible breakup, only to meet their perfect partner a couple months later.

If you listen to their stories, you might hear them say things like, "If I hadn't gone through what I did with my ex then I wouldn't appreciate what I have now".

Or, "If I met him sooner, I would have been a completely different person".

There is someone out there for everyone—even you.

It's just that some of them are still 'In the making'.

Trust that you will meet that special someone. In the meantime, keep focussing on becoming the best version of you.

When the time is right, the right one will come along.

The Only Thing You Need to Remember

You Are Amazing

Take yourself to a mirror and have a good look at the person staring back at you.

>This person is *brave.*
>This person is *strong.*
>This person is *worthy.*
>This person is *capable.*
>This person is *powerful.*
>This person is *beautiful.*
>This person is *confident.*
>This person is *incredible.*
>This person is *independent.*
>This person has *overcome a lot.*
>This person is *deserving of happiness.*
>This person is *taking control of her life.*
>This person is *amazing in so many ways.*

This person is **YOU**.

The End.

Printed in Great Britain
by Amazon